Nicholas Hurd

How to Get Started Making Money with an Online Business

A Blueprint for Making Money in the Digital Age

Createspace 2018

Limits of Liability and Disclaimer of Warrantee

Trademarks

Copyright Notice

How to Get Started Making Money with an Online Business

Looking to Start an Online Business

Here is your blueprint to get your online business started. It's based on years of working with small and medium sized business owners that have found success on the Internet.

You Will Discover

•How to Choose a Profitable Market

•What Kind of Product You Want to Offer

•What You Need for Your Online Presence

•How to Promote Your Online Products

•How You Get Paid!

•And Much, Much More

Índice

Step 1 – Choose a Market that's Profitable..........................5

Step 2 - Setting Up Your Online Presence..........................13

Step 3 – Promoting Your Products or Services...................17

There are a lot of benefits to starting an online business. It is flexible, it allows you to work from anywhere in the world, there is low-risk level, and it doesn't require a huge financial commitment, to begin with. However, starting an online business is no easy task. It requires proper planning, research, dedication, and commitment before one can start an online business and make money.

We at NiftyCart.com have put together this complete step-by-step guide which can enable you to get started with your online business and earn extra money.

Step 1 – Choose a Market that's Profitable

The first thing you need to do is to choose a market for your online business that will be profitable. It all begins with thorough planning. Consider various options, their pros & cons, before zeroing on a particular one. For better prospects, a SWOT [Strengths, Weaknesses, Opportunities, and Threats] analysis is also recommended.

After you are done with initial planning, it is the time to choose the market for your business. This is one of the biggest keys to success for every online business. The success of your online business will depend greatly on how you target your customers, which is something only possible if you choose your market carefully.

Having an understanding of the market will allow you to target your customers in the most effective way. You will get to know useful information related to your prospect customers i.e. their needs, wants, the time they spend online, and the ways you can reach them. Moreover, it will also enable you to understand the right words (content) that can trigger a positive response from your prospective customers.

Another thing you need to consider when choosing a market for your online business is the number of competitors in that particular market. The more competitors you have, there are more chances of the market having better prospects. However, making a presence in a market, which has more competitors, may prove to be difficult for a start-up. Your startup may also require more financing.

In order to create your niche in the market, it's important to evaluate the strategy that's employed by your competitors. Then you can come up with one, which will give your business a vital edge over your competitors. You will have to create value with your offerings to your prospect customers if you want to cut through the noise and carve your own place

Information Products

An easy, cost-effective, and profitable way to successfully run an online business is to sell information products. These products can come in all sort of formats i.e. pdf, video, audio etc. However, the main objective of such products should be to provide value to your customers.

People use the internet to search for easy guides, strategies, tips, and tricks to make their life better. This is where information products can come in handy. You can sell these products i.e. e-books, audio files, webinar etc. to them through Facebook, Twitter and your website and earn money.

Information products are relatively risk-free as they are cheap to create. All they require is your dedication, time, and energy. So if the information product, which you have created, fails, there will be no monetary loss.

For creating an information product that will give will value to your customers, you need to come up with innovative ideas for attracting them. The first thing to do while creating an information product is to find a problem, people are facing. Introduce your customers to the problems, and address with the solution you have created.

Here are some topics that are always available for a different approach:

•Weight loss

•Pet Care – for specific animals

•Exercise

You can research to find topics for your information product(s). Check out topics people are talking about online and in magazines. Discover what's trending on Twitter and in Facebook. What are the most read topics on Yahoo and other similar sites.

Another type of information product, if you have the appropriate skill, is teaching people how to do something, like:

•Playing guitar

•Playing Piano

•Photography

•Photo Editing

•Painting

•Anything people want to learn that you know how to do

One of the great things about this type of information product is you can do it as a subscription model. That means you supply a new lesson every week/month AND you collect money every month.

Another advantage of creating informative products is that they do not require any physical space for storage. You can use cloud based computing for storing them. However, make sure to have a backup.

The choice of which information product(s) you are going to sell depends on your skills. If you are good at writing, you can opt for e-books. Similarly, you can make videos or audios if you have the required skills. The selection of information products you will be selling also depend on the taste of the customers and the value they will derive from them.

Selling Your Crafts

If you are one of those people that are great with craft projects, the selling your crafts online can be a great source of additional income for you. One of the things that makes selling your crafts is they are unique. No one else has exactly the same product you do. That's a distinct advantage when it comes to selling online.

You can sell your crafts like:

•Jewelry

•Paintings

•Photos

•Knick Knacks

Selling Your Services Research

If you have expertise in a service that other people are looking for, like:

•Website design

•Creating Apps

•Creating Bots

•Graphic Art

•Writing Term Papers

•And so on

You can sell those services and many others. Even if your talents aren't one of those listed there are a LOT of other categories that people will pay you to do for them.

Physical Product Research

If you are contemplating the idea of selling physical products through your online business, there is a lot of research work to be done. It will require your time, effort, and dedication, in addition to hassles of storing and delivering the products. Despite all these hassles, selling products online can prove to be more profitable for your online business.

There are many physical product categories you can sell, including:

- Supplements

- Toys

- Computer Consumables (toner, ink, specialty paper, etc.)

- Electronics

There are various options that you can explore for selling products online. Let's have a look at different ways you can add products to your store and sell them to your customers.

White Label

With white label products, all the hassles of creating the products are eliminated. The process involves rebranding the products that are already produced by some other company. Various consumer products, electronics, software packages, and web applications etc. fall under white label products category.

With white label solution, there will be no concern and worry for the reseller to spend time and money on the development and research of the product(s). These products are time-saving. Instead of spending months (or years, in some cases), you will be able to offer your customers valuable products in no time and earn profits for your business.

It will require ample time and effort on your part to select the white label products that will reap in fruitful benefits for your business. On the other hand, planning for, and creating a product from scratch will take more time, effort, and money than you might have imagined. There are various aspects associated with creating your own products for your brand i.e. modeling, design, building, and testing. All these phases require human and capital resources. Therefore, you need to be equipped with adequate resources, if you are opting for making your products. All these hassles will be eliminated if you are opting for white label solution.

Drop Shipping

Drop shipping process includes taking orders for your online business. It is basically selling products, which you do not own. The orders that you have taken are forwarded to supplier or drop ship partners. Your supplier partners will ship the products, on your behalf, to your customers. The biggest advantage that is associated with drop shipping is that there is no need to for managing large inventory of goods.

Drop shipping poses a low risk and requires low start up cost. However, you may not earn a huge margin of profits initially as the profit margin is relatively low and there is high competition in this model of online business.

Inventory

Another option is to have a physical inventory with you for selling the goods. The option can prove to be profitable, but it requires dedicated and hard work to manage the inventory and shipment. You can buy the goods in bulk from wholesalers and resell them to the customers. The biggest benefit with inventory option is that it is a low-risk model. Since you are dealing with brands, which have already created value with customers, there are lesser chances of your business failures. However, there are certain cons associated with this model too. You will find plenty of other retailers selling the same products, which you have added to your store. Therefore, it can prove to be difficult for a newly emerging online store to position itself among the old players of the market.

Step 2 - Setting Up Your Online Presence

One of the first things you want to do is decide on a business name. I recommend that before you start ordering business cards, register the name with your county or state, you need to do one thing.

Your Domain Name

Is your business name, or a shortened version of it available as a dotCom. For example: yourbusinessname.com. If it's not available try to find variations of the name that you can get the dotCom for the name. There are other top level domains, like dotNet, dotCo, dotOrg, and so on. The challenge is that most people automatically go to dotCom.

The other potential issue if you can't get the dotCom is that someone else has it and may be using it. So, if you get yourbusinessname.net, for example, and someone else has yourbusinessname.com, guess who is going to get the visits

Another issue is you may not be able to get a Facebook page with yourbusinessname if someone else has it. And, I believe having your Facebook page in today's world is as important as having a website. It may even be more important!

NameCheap.com is a low cost domain registrar that I use and recommend.

Registering Your Business

Once you have a business name, you should register your business with your county or state government. Who you register with varies by state. The easiest thing to do to get started is register as a DBA (doing business as) so, it would be yourname DBA yourcompanyname. There are other business forms, like LLCs and Corporations, but the discussion of what is best for your business is beyond the scope of this book.

In addition, depending on your state's rules, you should register for a resale license. This allows you to charge sales tax for sales in your state. This is important if your state requires you to collect taxes on your sales. You could get in serious difficulties if you don't. Again, where and how to accomplish this in your state is beyond the scope of this book.

Setting Up

After deciding on the information products and physical products you are going to offer your customers through your online business, it is the time to set up your online presence. You need to make people aware of the products you are offering and give them a reason to shop from your store.

The first thing, in order to set up your online presence, is to set up a Facebook page. Facebook has emerged as an outstanding social media platform for spreading the name of your business. Almost everyone these days has their Facebook accounts. Therefore, it can be termed as the most reliable platform to set up the online presence of your business as it allows a greater reach.

Through the Facebook page, you have created; you can target your potential customers directly. More important, creating a Facebook page is easy. You won't have to spend money from your pocket to create the page. All it requires is a couple of minutes and you are good to go. If you are not a graphic artist, I recommend you hire someone to create your Facebook Cover image.

In order to turn your prospects into long term customers, you need to target them with attractive content through your Facebook page. By providing them with valuable information, you will be able to capture their interest and target them accordingly. You can also use animated graphics, videos or audios to provide value to the customers. However, make sure you aren't cluttering their feed with images and animations.

Your Website

Once you have created an identity on social media platform, the next step is to think about setting up a website. In today's world with social media it's not the requirement it once was. Setting up a website can be expensive if you are not doing it yourself. You might consider not setting up a website until you are successful on Facebook, for example.

When you are ready to set up your website, I recommend using WordPress. It has many features that will do anything you want to do. And, can be a DIY project. There are other options if you have specific reasons to NOT use WordPress. WordPress is the easiest to maintain after it is set up and has thousands of plugins that make your website work for you promoting your business.

It is important to note that your website and social media profiles are a direct reflection of the value you are offering to your customers. If your website is poorly designed or you are not handling your Facebook page efficiently, customers will feel reluctant to order products from your business. Therefore, get a website with the attractive design even if you have to pay some extra bucks for it. Make is easy to use for the customers so that they can buy the products instantly without going through any hassles. There should be no more than two clicks between them checking the details of the products they desire and the checkout process. A lengthy checkout process can frustrate the customers.

In short, setting up your online presence will help you to reach a wider audience and spread the name of your brand. The gist of this step is to make your website customer-friendly so that they shop in a hassle-free manner from your online store.

Step 3 – Promoting Your Products or Services

The last, but the most important, step for setting up your online business is to promote the products and/or services you are offering. Here are some different ways you can do this:

An effective way to promote your brand's offering is to direct excess? traffic to your website. You can do so by placing Adwords ads based on keywords related to your products or services. This will help to enhance your website ranking. The more customers visiting your website, the more there are chances of the success of your online business. Keyword placing is an important tool for the SEO of your website; hence, special attention needs to be paid for this.

Adwords

Adwords display ads are another effective way to driving traffic to your website, in order to enhance your sales. They will help to direct your prospective customers to your website. When a prospect clicks on the display ad, they will be directed to your website; hence, you will enjoy a greater traffic and there will be brighter chances of your goods being sold in greater numbers. You will have to spend money on this promotional tactic, but the outcome i.e. the enhanced sales will definitely be worth the money you will spend on it.

Facebook

As discussed above, Facebook is one of the major platforms to market and promote your products. However, posting on your brand's Facebook page alone will not help you to grow your customer base. You will need to promote your Facebook posts in order to reach to a wider range of audience. For this purpose, you will need to keep your page active. Facebook is also offering cheap models for post promotion. They will charge you some money and your posts will be promoted across the feeds of various users even if they haven't liked your page.

You can also use the Facebook platform for advertising your brand. Apart from post promotion, Facebook is also offering advertisement models. By advertising your brand on Facebook, you will be able to grow your community as more and more people will get aware of your brand and its offerings. Facebook ads, due to their effectiveness, have become quite popular with the digital marketers. For better outcome, you can create video ads and Facebook will post them on the feeds of the users.

Instagram

Apart from Facebook, you can also use other social media platforms for marketing and promotional purpose. As per statistics, Instagram has 700 million monthly active users. Therefore, it has emerged out to be a popular platform for the digital marketers to promote their products. If you are an Instagram user, you must have noticed various ads appearing on your feed. These ads link directly to the brand's website. You can also take advantage of this popular platform to market and products the products and/or services you are offering.

Twitter

In addition to Facebook and Instagram, Twitter is another popular social media platform used by the internet users. Due to its popularity, it allows marketers to reach a wider audience to promote their products. This platform can prove to be profitable for the individuals who are new to operating an online business as they can avail the extensive benefits of this platform and spread a name of their brand. They can use the hashtag (#) feature of the microblogging website Twitter in order to "trend" the name of their brand.

Messenger

Messenger can also prove to be an effective tool for promoting and marketing your products. It allows a one-to-one communication with the prospective customer. With Messenger, you can answer the queries of your customers and provide them effective solutions. Moreover, this can also play a handy part in getting the feedback of the products and/or services, which you are offering.

Email

Many people neglect E-mail marketing, thinking of it as an obsolete way to promote the products. However, that is only a myth as e-mail marketing is still known to reap profitable benefits for the marketers. You can send an e-mail with useful, meaningful, effective, and quality content to promote your products to the prospective customers who have signed up for your email list. With your content, you can add a small yet effective call to action in the end for driving the recipient of the email to your website.

In this cut throat competition in the digital market, it has become important for every business, whether new or old, to use social media platforms to market their products. If you want to grow your customer base and enhance your sales, you need to be active on all the major social media platforms.

In order to promote your products and/or services from your online business across various social media networks, you can use integrated software that is available to be downloaded from the web. This software will allow you to simultaneously post your quality and useful content on different social media platforms. Moreover, through this software, you can also schedule your posts and enjoy various other extensive features.

Content

Content marketing is another useful way to promote your products. For this purpose, you need to come up with quality content which will compel the internet users to buy products from your brand. You can use the content that you have created in your social media feeds and email marketing.

Moreover, you can also hire bloggers to write content for your brand and publish them on their blogs so that more and more people could visit your website and purchase your products.

Another way to use your content and get visitors to your site is through QUUU. It's a site that allows owners of other websites to use pieces of your content with links to the full document on your website. If you have good content it can deliver lots of visitors.

You can get content for your site from QUUU as well. It's the other side of shared content. You get quality content for your site, drawing visitors in, and get sales from their visits.

YouTube

Creating YouTube videos can be a time-consuming task, but it can prove to be a successful promotional tactic for your online brand. You can either create YouTube videos by yourself or hire online services for this purpose. The content of these videos must be well thought out. They should be created according to the taste of your target customers. You can integrate your brand's YouTube channel with your social media platforms for promoting the videos. This will allow increased views on your videos which will result in a higher lead generation.

There you go, now that you are aware of all the key steps to get started with your online business, you shouldn't waste any more time and create your plan for a successful and profitable online business.

Getting the Sale

You have all the pieces now it comes down to getting your customer to open his or her wallet and give you the money. To do this you need a shopping cart.

Shopping carts fall into two basic categories: Hosted and Self Hosted

Hosted Shopping Carts

Self-hosted shopping carts are carts that are built into your website.

There are several advantages to self-hosted carts:

•They are built into your design and are part of your look and feel

•They are easy to maintain as they are a part of your site

On the other hand, there are several disadvantages to self-hosted carts:

•You must have a SSL security certificate for your site

•You must be PCI compliant (payment card industry)

•Your site must be scanned regularly to confirm it's secure

•Can't sell on your Facebook page

Hosted Shopping Carts

Advantages of Hosted shopping carts:

•They are secure, meet PCI compliance and are tested regularly

•They are easy to set up because, generally you are just adding your products to a database

•Can sell easily right on your Facebook page

Disadvantage of Hosted shopping carts:

•They may not match exactly the look and feel of your website

•They may be more expensive than self hosted carts

•May have fewer options than self hosted

Finally...

When you've done all that, then you need to have a way for people to pay for your products or services. NiftyCart.com gives you a simple way to get started selling online. You can have your products ready for sale in 5 minutes or less. You don't even need a website to get started; you can sell from your Facebook page. And, you can start accepting credit and debit cards immediately.

In addition, as your online business grows, you will find tools that will help you manage and automate your business. You'll find tools like:

Automatic digital downloads of your information products

Interface to email autoresponders so you can keep in touch with your customers

Automatic sales accounting to your QuickBooks account Notification of abandoned carts with automatic follow ups

Customer accounts and remembered orders so your customers can shop at your online store more easily

Coupons to give your customers a reason to return for more purchases

Your products/services will display properly on any device PC, tablet or phone and much more.

I hope the information in this book has helped you get started on your exciting journey into selling online, and remember, if you are serious about starting this new online business, we are offering a personal one-on-one consultation with our founder and CEO Nicholas Hurd to start you off in the right direction for you. For more information, go to http://www.niftycart.com/consultation.html.

Check out www.niftycart.com and get started selling online today!

Nicks Bio

Nicholas Hurd is the CEO of Litening Software, Inc. He has been helping small and medium sized companies achieve financial success in starting and running their businesses for more than 30 years.

Nicholas has a Bachelor of Science in Marketing from California State University East Bay. In addition he has 2 certifications from Microsoft, Solution Developer and Database Analyst.